THE POWER OF KINDNESS

BY ABBY COLICH

BLUE OWL
BOOKS

TIPS FOR CAREGIVERS

Social and emotional learning (SEL) helps children manage emotions, create and achieve goals, maintain relationships, learn how to feel empathy, and make good decisions. The SEL approach will help children establish positive habits in communication, cooperation, and decision-making. By incorporating SEL in early reading, children will be better equipped to build confidence and foster positive peer networks.

BEFORE READING

Talk to the reader about what it means to be kind.

Discuss: Think of a time someone was kind to you. What did they say or do that was kind? How did it make you feel?

AFTER READING

Talk about the many benefits of practicing kindness.

Discuss: Why is it important to be kind? What is one way to show kindness?

SEL GOAL

Children may have a difficult time understanding the benefits of showing and receiving kindness. Explain to children that certain actions can trigger reactions in the brain. These reactions can affect how they feel in their mind and body. Being kind and being shown kindness can help them feel good and make their lives better.

TABLE OF CONTENTS

DONATION BOX

CHAPTER 1

WHAT KINDNESS LOOKS LIKE

Have you ever helped a friend? Has someone helped you or shared something with you? These are examples of kindness.

You can practice kindness every day. You can smile at a neighbor. You can give someone a **compliment** like, "You are a good friend."

You can also show your **community** kindness. How? You can collect food and **donate** it to people in need. You can also pick up trash. This is kind to your community and the planet.

Have you ever told yourself you can do something that seems hard? That's being kind to yourself!

CHAPTER 2

THE BENEFITS OF KINDNESS

When you are kind to others, it makes them feel good. It also helps you feel connected to them.

Kindness can make people's lives better. It helps communities and the world, too. Practicing kindness is also good for your mind and body!

Have you ever felt warm and bubbly after being nice to someone? Researchers found that showing kindness releases dopamine in our brains.

Dopamine is a **neurotransmitter**. It is made in the hypothalamus and midbrain. It activates the brain's **reward system**. This means you feel good when you are kind. You want to keep doing it.

RANDOM ACTS OF KINDNESS

Random acts of kindness are unplanned. These include holding the door for a stranger or picking up something someone dropped.

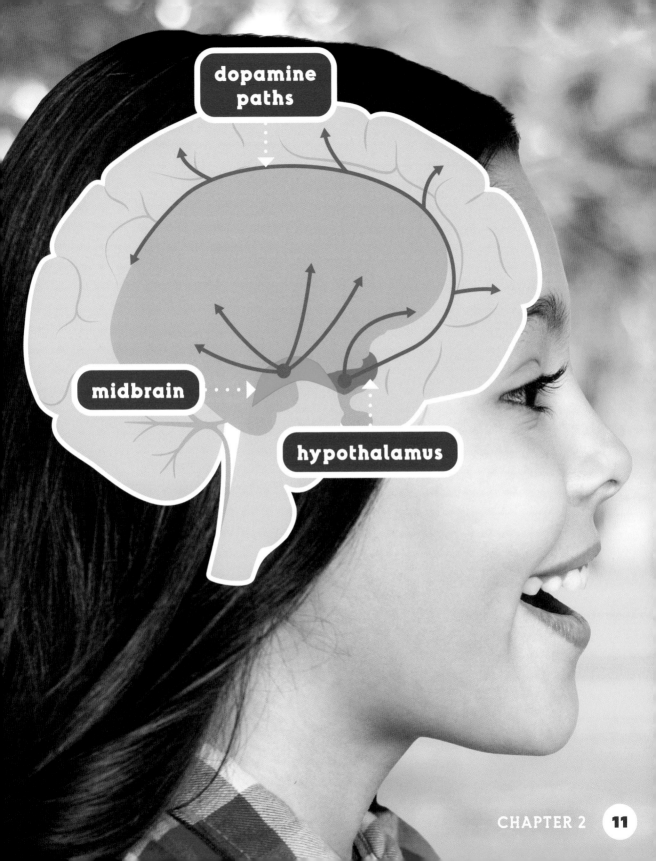

dopamine
paths

midbrain

hypothalamus

hypothalamus

brain stem

pituitary gland

Showing kindness boosts serotonin. This is another neurotransmitter. It is made in the brain stem. It helps put you in a good mood.

Your brain also releases oxytocin. Oxytocin is another neurotransmitter. It is made in the hypothalamus. It is stored in the pituitary gland. Oxytocin travels through your body. It helps you feel connected to others. It can make you more trusting and friendly.

Tina is new at school. Adam and Leah see her eating lunch alone. They decide to eat with Tina every day. This makes everyone feel good.

When you are kind, your body releases **endorphins**. Endorphins help you feel good and less **stressed**.

Cortisol is a **hormone** your body makes when you are stressed. Too much cortisol can be harmful. Practicing kindness can lower it. Being kind helps you feel calm. Josie is stressed about her homework. She sees that Mac looks stressed, too. She asks if he wants to work together. They feel calmer.

ALWAYS BE KIND

Scientists found that we do not experience **benefits** by only being kind once. People who practice kindness often get the most benefits.

CHAPTER 3

HOW TO PRACTICE KINDNESS

Being kind benefits you and the people around you. You can choose to be kind in any situation, even when it seems hard.

Look for times you can show kindness. Start by making a list of all the ways you could be nice and helpful to others. Soon you will start thinking of more ways to show kindness.

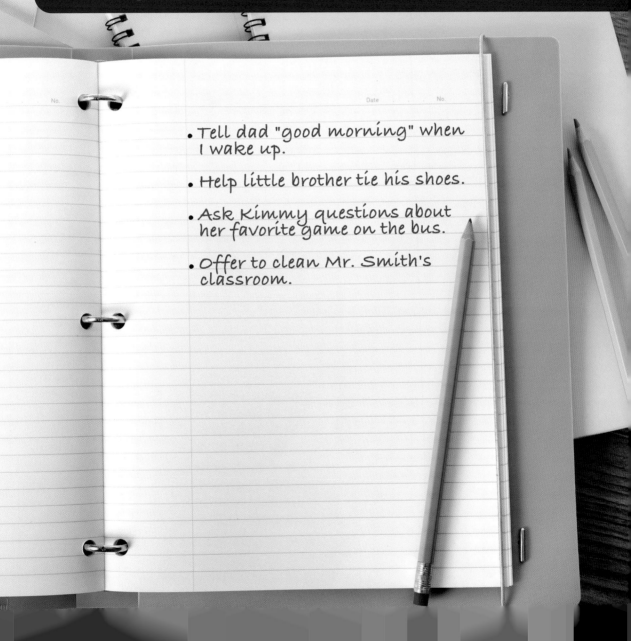

- Tell dad "good morning" when I wake up.
- Help little brother tie his shoes.
- Ask Kimmy questions about her favorite game on the bus.
- Offer to clean Mr. Smith's classroom.

Do you see someone who looks upset? Ask if they need a friend to talk to. Then, try to show them **empathy**. Think about how they are feeling. Learning empathy helps you show kindness to others.

Gabby sees that Helen looks sad. She asks her what is wrong. Helen is upset because she lost her favorite book. Gabby tells her about a time she lost something. She knows how Helen feels. She shows her empathy and kindness.

Spreading kindness to others and the world around you can help everyone feel good. Make sure you are kind to yourself, too. Take time to **meditate** and relax your mind. Or spend some time alone to recharge. Showing yourself and others kindness makes the world a better place.

BALANCED KINDNESS

Sometimes people focus more on others than themselves. Being kind to others is important. But you need to take care of yourself, too. If you feel tired or anxious, take some time alone for a break. Find ways to show yourself kindness.

GOALS AND TOOLS

GROW WITH GOALS

Kindness has many benefits for others, the world around you, and yourself.

Goal: Write kind notes to your family. Write down what you like about each family member or something they do well. Leave the notes where they will see them.

Goal: Model kindness. Ask if you and your classmates can do a playground cleanup with younger students. You will model kindness for the younger students while showing kindness to your community.

Goal: Spread kindness to everyone. Give a compliment to someone you don't know.

TRY THIS!

Make a kindness calendar. Get a calendar. On each day, write something you can do to be kind to yourself, another person, the planet, or your community. Then, cross the ideas off as you complete them. You don't have to do them in order or on the exact day. But use the calendar as inspiration to do something kind each day. It will help you brainstorm ways you can be kind. Then, start again at the beginning of the next month.

GLOSSARY

benefits
Things that produce good or helpful results or effects or that promote well-being.

community
A place and the people who live in it.

compliment
To say something kind about someone or something.

donate
To give something to a charity or cause.

empathy
The ability to understand and share the emotions and experiences of others.

endorphins
Substances created by the brain that reduce pain and cause pleasant feelings.

hormone
A chemical substance made by the body that affects the way your body grows, develops, and functions.

meditate
To think deeply and quietly.

neurotransmitter
A chemical messenger in the body that sends information from one neuron to another.

reward system
Parts of the brain that activate whenever you do something that makes you feel good.

stressed
Experiencing mental or emotional strain.

TO LEARN MORE

FACT SURFER

Finding more information is as easy as 1, 2, 3.

1. Go to www.factsurfer.com

2. Enter "**thepowerofkindness**" into the search box.

3. Choose your book to see a list of websites.

INDEX

Blue Owl Books are published by Jump!, 5357 Penn Avenue South, Minneapolis, MN 55419, www.jumplibrary.com

Library of Congress Cataloging-in-Publication Data

Names: Colich, Abby, author.
Title: The power of kindness / by Abby Colich.
Description: Minneapolis, MN: Jump!, Inc., [2024]
Series: The power of positivity | Includes index.
Audience: Ages 7–10
Identifiers: LCCN 2023033233 (print)
LCCN 2023033234 (ebook)
ISBN 9798889966890 (hardcover)
ISBN 9798889966906 (paperback)
ISBN 9798889966913 (ebook)
Subjects: LCSH: Kindness—Juvenile literature.
Classification: LCC BJ1533.K5 C635 2024 (print)
LCC BJ1533.K5 (ebook)
DDC 177/.7—dc23/eng/20230907
LC record available at https://lccn.loc.gov/2023033233
LC ebook record available at https://lccn.loc.gov/2023033234

Editor: Katie Chanez
Designer: Emma Almgren-Bersie
Content Consultant: Megan Kraemer, MSW, LICSW

Photo Credits: FAMILY STOCK/Shutterstock, cover; sonyae/iStock, 1; White bear studio/Shutterstock, 3; SolStock/iStock, 4; kali9/iStock, 5; andreswd/iStock, 6–7; nirat/iStock, 8; Chayantorn/iStock, 9; Roman Samborskyi/Shutterstock, 10–11 (foreground); mangpor2004/Shutterstock, 10–11 (background); Africa Studio/Shutterstock, 12–13 (foreground); nicepix/Shutterstock, 12–13 (background); PeopleImages.com - Yuri A/Shutterstock, 14–15; Kdonmuang/Shutterstock, 16; David Franklin/Shutterstock, 17; SeventyFour/Shutterstock, 18–19; Pixel-Shot/Shutterstock, 20–21.

Printed in the United States of America at Corporate Graphics in North Mankato, Minnesota.